John Kember

# More Piano Sight-Reading 3

## Déchiffrage pour le piano 3
## Neue Vom-Blatt-Spiel-Übungen auf dem Klavier 3

*Additional material for piano solo*
*Pieces pour piano solo*
*Zusätzliche Stücke für Klavier*

ED 13635
ISMN: 979-0-2201-1841-8
ISBN: 978-1-84761-324-0

www.schott-music.com

Mainz · London · Madrid · New York · Paris · Prague · Tokyo · Toronto
© 2015 SCHOTT MUSIC Ltd, London · Printed in Germany

ED 13635

British Library Cataloguing-in-Publication Data.
A catalogue record for this book is available from the British Library
ISMN: 979-0-2201-1841-8
ISBN: 978-1-84761-324-0

French translation: Michaëla Rubi
German translation: Heike Brühl
Music setting and page layout by Bev Wilson
Cover design by www.adamhaystudio.com
Printed in Germany S&Co.9076

# Contents
## Sommaire/Inhalt

# Preface

Although pianists rarely get the opportunity to perform in an orchestra or other large ensemble, the piano is remarkably versatile in the forms and styles of music in which it can play.

Apart from the vast library of music written for the instrument over some 350 years and by most of the world's greatest composers, there are other outlets for the pianist to explore which offer the opportunity to perform with other musicians. There is also a wealth of music written for piano duet or two pianos that can provide both enjoyment and the pleasure of performing with another pianist.

Accompanying is an art in itself and demands the ability to listen and adapt, following rather than leading. It gives access to a new and varied repertoire with both instrumentalists and singers, small ensembles and choirs, and the world of musical theatre. Arrangements and transcriptions of music from other genres can provide an entirely new and exciting challenge and offer a chance to explore an alternative repertoire.

The pianist can be called upon to read chords not only with traditional notation, but with a variety of signs and symbols. These are introduced in the final section of this book with introductions to the figured bass – as found in Baroque music, Roman numerals, as found in the study of harmony, and with chord names as is common practice in pop and jazz music. All these are, or can be, part of the 'complete pianist's' armoury and further add to the opportunities open to the player.

The main topic of this book, however, is to study the art of fingering. It aims to help the pianist to understand how best to move around the keyboard with the minimum of movement and to negotiate the black and white notes comfortably and economically, in preparation for when faced with music written with either limited fingering or none at all. At this point you will be expected to cope unaided.

## To the pupil: why sight-reading?

When faced with a new or unfamiliar piece, we have learnt to consider the rhythm first, then to observe the key, time signature, accidentals required, general shape, style and dynamics. It is essential to scan the piece for anything unusual by looking at every note, however briefly.

Now we need to add another dimension – that of fingering. Starting a piece is rather like embarking on a journey. We need to know where we are heading and by which route. This might involve studying a road map first so as to know where and when to turn.

The pianist too has to look at the fingering and be aware of where the hand position will need to change. To begin with we are guided through this process by the numbers given, each indicating a necessary hand position change. If we should choose to ignore these we will soon run into difficulties! Fingering is added only after considerable thought, and makes use of the needs to negotiate the black notes in any given key and for the comfort and ease of the performer. Fingering is determined mainly with the key in mind and knowledge of what is coming next. You may already have noticed that this assistance gradually reduces as pieces become more complex with the use of chords which would otherwise require detailed numbering. Some essential guidance may be given, but you will gradually be left to fend for yourself, and eventually manage your fingering efficiently as you go along.

This book aims to assist you in understanding the logic of fingering. When it comes to playing with chords it becomes impractical and over fussy to put in any other that absolutely essential fingering. If you play both quicker and more complex pieces employing patterns, scale and arpeggio figures (e.g. Bach's Two-part Inventions) you will find that you may observe the patterns but your main guide to fluent playing will be to read those essential numbers. Failure to do so will inevitably lead to a slip of some sort.

It is recommended that you study fingering in pieces while you still have the opportunity and not take it for granted, fail to see the reasoning behind it, or ignore it!

In this book we have attempted to break this focus on fingering down by first showing where a 5 note hand position needs to change, then by giving fingering for part of the piece with the recommendation that you use a pencil to prepare the remaining bars in a similar manner. This is done firstly with 2 part pieces, then with the introduction of 2 note chords in one hand or the other, then with 3 note chords, and SATB voicings. The final section will contain a mixture of all these. Various styles will be encountered including syncopated, jazz and swing style, and some chromatic, modal and atonal pieces. In these pieces careful reading is encouraged as they may not sound quite as you expect.

Finally, as the aim of learning is to prepare you for independence and equip you to choose for yourself what you wish to play, then understanding fingering and becoming skilled at reading ahead and anticipating the need to change position will prove beneficial. Much of the advanced repertoire give little or no guidance on fingering, so the more experienced player needs a thorough understanding of its practical uses, and the ability to prepare it themselves.

There are 8 sections in this book each gradually building to instil both understanding and experience in appreciating the principles of planning fingering. This will enable the player to cope in readiness for the day when little or no fingering assistance is offered and the player will need to 'see ahead' and be prepared to use the most economical and comfortable way to proceed in order to give a fluent performance, trusting in knowledge and experience rather than luck.

**Section 1** begins by helping the player 'see' 5 finger hand positions and select the best finger to start each phrase with. It goes on to show how, based on the scale fingering, this can be achieved with minimal movement. The use of a pencil to help 'plan ahead' is highly recommended. All examples are in two parts.

**Section 2** Fingering suggestions are only given at the start of each two-part piece. Players are again strongly recommended to plan ahead, using a pencil, before any part is played. The importance of planning ahead for the octave leaps is also emphasised. Styles including swing and ragtime, and whole-tone tonality will be encountered.

**Section 3** consists of generally longer two-part pieces with some help given only for the first few bars. From then on it will have to be planned carefully before attempting to play.

**Section 4** introduces two-note chords concentrating particularly on 3rds, 6ths and octaves.

**Section 5** introduces three-note chords and the best options for fingering them, as well as keys with up to four sharps and flats.

**Section 6** concentrates on playing four-note chords (SATB).

**Section 7** employs a variety of styles and tonalities.

**Section 8** gives opportunities to learn about playing from chord symbols including roman numerals (as used in the study of harmony), figured bass (as found in much Baroque music) and chord symbols ( as found in jazz and popular music).

# Préface

Bien que les pianistes aient rarement l'occasion de jouer dans un orchestre ou dans une autre formation importante, le piano est un instrument polyvalent adapté à toutes sortes de formes et de styles musicaux différents.

Outre le vaste répertoire de musique écrite pour piano depuis plus de 350 ans par les plus grands compositeurs du monde, d'autres terrains d'exploration s'offrent aux pianistes qui leur permettent de jouer avec d'autres musiciens. Il existe aussi une abondance de musique écrite pour piano à quatre mains ou pour deux pianos, à même de procurer à la fois de la satisfaction et le plaisir de jouer à plusieurs.

L'accompagnement est un art à part entière et implique véritablement la capacité d'écouter et de s'adapter, de suivre plutôt que de mener. Il donne accès à un répertoire nouveau et varié pour instrumentistes et chanteurs, petits ensembles et chœurs ainsi qu'à tout l'univers du théâtre musical. Les arrangements et transcriptions de musiques appartenant à d'autres genres permettent de relever des défis totalement nouveaux et stimulants, et offrent la possibilité d'explorer un autre type de répertoire.

Le pianiste peut être amené à lire des accords non seulement en notation traditionnelle, mais dans toute une variété de signes et de symboles. Ces derniers sont abordés dans la dernière partie de notre ouvrage, avec une introduction à la basse figurée telle qu'on la trouve dans la musique baroque, aux chiffres romains rencontrés notamment dans l'étude de l'harmonie, et aux dénominations d'accords courantes dans la musique pop et dans le jazz. Toutes ces pratiques font partie, ou peuvent faire partie du « parfait petit équipement » du pianiste et lui permettent ensuite d'être ouvert à toutes les opportunités offertes.

Toutefois, le sujet principal de cet ouvrage est l'étude de l'art des doigtés. Il vise à permettre au pianiste de comprendre comment se déplacer efficacement sur le clavier, en faisant un minimum de mouvements, et de négocier les touches noires et blanches le plus confortablement et avec la plus grande économie possibles, pour se préparer à aborder au mieux les partitions, y compris lorsqu'elles comportent peu de doigtés, voire pas du tout. À terme, vous devriez être capables de vous en sortir sans aucune aide.

## À l'élève : Pourquoi le déchiffrage

Lorsque nous sommes confrontés à un morceau nouveau ou peu familier, nous avons appris à nous pencher d'abord sur le rythme, puis à observer l'armure, la mesure, les altérations accidentelles, la ligne générale, le style et les nuances. Il est essentiel de passer la pièce en revue à la recherche de tout élément inhabituel en s'arrêtant sur chaque note, même brièvement.

À présent, nous avons besoin d'ajouter une autre dimension – celle des doigtés. L'approche d'un nouveau morceau peut être comparée à un départ en voyage. Nous avons besoin de savoir où nous allons et par quel chemin. Cela peut impliquer l'étude d'une carte routière afin de savoir où et quand bifurquer.

Le pianiste lui aussi doit se soucier des doigtés et être conscient des endroits où il devra changer de position des mains. Au départ, nous sommes guidés dans ce processus par les chiffres proposés, chacun indiquant la nécessité d'un changement de position des mains. Choisir de les ignorer nous expose rapidement des difficultés ! Les doigtés sont le fruit d'une mûre réflexion et répondent à la nécessité de négocier les notes noires dans n'importe quelle tonalité de manière confortable et aisée pour l'interprète. Ils sont déterminés principalement par la tonalité et la connaissance de ce qui arrive ensuite. Vous aurez peut-être déjà remarqué que plus les pièces deviennent difficiles, avec la présence d'accords requérant généralement un chiffrage détaillé, plus cette aide diminue. Au-delà des quelques lignes de conduites essentielles énoncées ici, vous serez petit à petit livrés à vous-mêmes et au fur et à mesure que vous progresserez, saurez finalement négocier efficacement vos doigtés de manière autonome.

Cet ouvrage est destiné à vous aider à comprendre la logique des doigtés. Lorsqu'il s'agit de jouer en accords, la situation se complique souvent inutilement lorsqu'on essaye d'utiliser autre chose que le doigté absolument essentiel. Si vous jouez des pièces à la fois plus rapides et plus complexes utilisant des formules, des figures d'arpèges et de gammes (par ex. les *Inventions à deux voix* de Bach), vous vous rendrez compte que vous aurez conscience de ces formules, mais que ce qui vous guidera davantage pour une plus grande fluidité sera de lire ces fameux chiffres essentiels. Ne pas le faire conduirait inévitablement à une erreur d'une nature ou d'une autre.

Nous recommandons d'étudier les doigtés dans les morceaux que vous jouez tant que vous en avez encore la possibilité et de ne pas les considérer comme acquis, ni négliger le raisonnement qui les sous-tend ou les ignorer !

Dans cet ouvrage, nous avons tenté de vaincre cette focalisation sur les doigtés en montrant tout d'abord où les changements de position de la main sont nécessaires, puis en indiquant les doigtés de certaines parties du morceau en recommandant d'utiliser un crayon pour préparer les mesures restantes de manière similaire. Cela s'applique tout d'abord à des pièces à deux voix, puis sont introduits progressivement des accords de 2 notes à une main ou à l'autre, ensuite des accords de 3 notes et enfin une harmonisation à quatre voix SATB. La partie finale propose un mélange de toutes ces formules. Vous rencontrerez différents styles, y compris des styles syncopés de jazz et de swing, et quelques pièces chromatiques, modales et atonales. Nous encourageons une lecture soigneuse de ces dernières, car elles peuvent ne pas sonner du tout comme on s'y attendrait.

Enfin, le but de l'apprentissage étant de vous préparer à être indépendants et de vous équiper pour vous permettre de choisir vous-même ce que vous souhaitez jouer, la compréhension et l'acquisition des compétences de lecture « en avance » et d'anticipation des changements de positions nécessaires s'avéreront bénéfiques. Une grande partie du répertoire de niveau avancé ne comprendra que très peu de doigtés, voire aucun, afin que les instrumentistes les plus expérimentés fassent appel à une compréhension profonde de l'usage pratique des doigtés et acquièrent la capacité de les concevoir eux-mêmes.

L'ouvrage comprend huit parties progressives, permettant de à la fois d'approfondir la compréhension théorique et de renforcer la pratique des principes de planification des doigtés. Cela permettra à l'instrumentiste de se préparer pour le jour où il n'y aura que peu ou pas du tout d'aide en termes de doigtés et où il aura besoin d'anticiper et d'être prêt à utiliser les procédés les plus confortables et les plus économiques pour donner une interprétation fluide en se fiant à ses connaissances et à son expérience plutôt qu'à la chance.

**La section 1** commence par aider l'instrumentiste à « visualiser » les positions des mains et à sélectionner le meilleur doigt pour commencer chaque phrase. Elle poursuit en montrant comment y parvenir avec un minimum de mouvements en se fondant sur le doigté de la gamme. L'utilisation d'un crayon pour favoriser l'anticipation est fortement recommandée.
Tous les exemples sont à deux voix.

Dans **la section 2**, les suggestions de doigtés sont indiquées uniquement au début de chaque morceau à deux voix. Les interprètes sont à nouveau incités à anticiper avant de jouer quoi que ce soit, en s'aidant d'un crayon. L'importance de l'anticipation des sauts d'octaves est également soulignée. On y rencontre également des styles différents, incluant le swing et le ragtime ainsi que la gamme par tons.

**La section 3** consiste en pièces à deux voix généralement plus longues avec une aide seulement sur les quelques premières mesures. Ensuite, il faudra prévoir soigneusement les doigtés avant de commencer à jouer.

**La section 4** introduit les accords de deux notes en se concentrant particulièrement sur les tierces, les sixtes et les octaves.

**La section 5** introduit les accords de trois notes et les meilleures options de doigtés correspondantes, ainsi que les tonalités à quatre bémols et quatre dièses.

**La section 6** se concentre sur les accords de quatre notes (SATB).

**La section 7** fait appel à toute une variété de styles et de tonalités.

**La section 8** donne l'occasion d'apprendre à réaliser des accords à partir de symboles incluant les chiffres romains (comme dans l'étude de l'harmonie), la basse figurée (comme on la trouve dans la musique baroque) et les symboles d'accords (comme dans le jazz et la musique populaire).

# Vorwort

Obwohl Pianisten nur selten die Gelegenheit haben, in einem Orchester oder großen Ensemble zu spielen, ist das Klavier in Bezug auf musikalische Formen und Stilrichtungen unglaublich vielseitig.

Außer der umfassenden Spielliteratur, die in den letzten 350 Jahren und von den weltbesten Komponisten für Klavier geschrieben wurde, gibt es für Pianisten auch viele Möglichkeiten, mit anderen Musikern zu spielen. Es gibt z. B. zahlreiche Klavierduette und Stücke für zwei Klaviere, die man mit einem anderen Pianisten spielen kann und die viel Spaß machen.

Begleiten ist eine Kunst für sich und erfordert die Fähigkeit zuzuhören und sich anzupassen, d. h. eher zu folgen als zu führen. Es bietet einen Zugang zu einem neuen, vielseitigen Repertoire sowohl mit Instrumentalisten als auch mit Sängern, kleinen Ensembles und Chören sowie der Welt des Musiktheaters. Arrangements und Bearbeitungen von Musikstücken aus anderen Genres können eine ganz neue Herausforderung darstellen und bieten die Gelegenheit, ein anderes Repertoire kennen zu lernen.

Es kann sein, dass man als Pianist Akkorde lesen können muss, die nicht nur in der herkömmlichen Notation, sondern mithilfe verschiedener Zeichen und Symbolen dargestellt werden. Diese werden im letzten Kapitel dieses Buches vorgestellt: der Generalbass aus der Barockmusik, römische Ziffern aus der Harmonielehre und Akkordbezeichnungen aus der Pop- und Jazzmusik. All diese Zeichen sind bzw. sollten Bestandteile der Ausrüstung eines guten Pianisten sein und eröffnen ihm weitere Möglichkeiten.

Das Hauptthema dieses Buches ist jedoch die Kunst des Fingersatzes. Das Ziel des Buches ist zu lernen, wie man sich mit minimalem Aufwand auf der Tastatur bewegen und bequem und ökonomisch zwischen den schwarzen und weißen Tasten wechseln kann. Dies dient der Vorbereitung auf Musikstücke, die entweder nur einen spärlichen oder überhaupt keinen Fingersatz enthalten. In diesem Fall muss man dann ohne Hilfe zurechtkommen.

## An den Schüler: Warum Vom-Blatt-Spiel?

Wenn du ein neues Stück spielen möchtest, hast du gelernt, zuerst auf den Rhythmus zu achten, dann auf die Tonart, die Taktart, die erforderlichen Vorzeichen sowie Melodieverlauf, Artikulation und dynamische Zeichen. Es ist wichtig, das Stück auf ungewöhnliche Dinge abzusuchen, indem du dir jede Note anschaust, und sei es auch noch so kurz.

Jetzt müssen wir einen weiteren Aspekt hinzufügen: den Fingersatz. Ein Stück zum ersten Mal zu spielen ist wie der Beginn einer Reise. Wir müssen wissen, wohin wir reisen möchten und welche Route wir nehmen wollen. Daher müssen wir vielleicht zuerst auf einer Straßenkarte nachschauen, wo und wann wir abbiegen müssen.

Der Pianist muss sich zuerst den Fingersatz ansehen und sich bewusst machen, wo die Handposition verändert werden muss. Zunächst weiß man durch die angegebenen Zahlen, wann ein Wechsel erforderlich ist. Wenn man die Zahlen ignoriert, gerät man schon bald in Schwierigkeiten! Ein Fingersatz wird erst nach reiflicher Überlegung hinzugefügt und erfüllt die Aufgabe, die Noten jeder Tonart zu bewerkstelligen und es dem Pianisten so leicht und bequem wie möglich zu machen. Fingersätze werden hauptsächlich durch die Tonart und das Wissen, was als nächstes kommt, bestimmt. Vielleicht ist dir schon aufgefallen, dass der hilfreiche Fingersatz allmählich immer spärlicher wird, wenn die Stücke komplexer werden und Akkorde enthalten, die eigentlich einen detaillierten Fingersatz erfordern würden. Zwar gibt es dann noch die nötigsten Hinweise, aber nach und nach musst du dich alleine durchschlagen und dir beim Spielen einen eigenen Fingersatz ausdenken.

Dieses Buch soll dir helfen, die Logik des Fingersatzes zu verstehen. Beim Spielen mit Akkorden ist es unpraktisch und übertrieben, einen anderen Fingersatz als den absolut notwendigen anzugeben. Wenn du sowohl schnellere als auch komplexere Stücke spielst, die Akkord-Pattern, Tonleiterfiguren und Arpeggien enthalten (z. B. Bachs zweistimmige Inventionen), wirst du feststellen, dass du zwar die Pattern beachtest, dein wichtigster Wegweiser zum flüssigen Spiel jedoch die Zahlen sind. Wenn du sie nicht lesen kannst, machst du zwangsläufig irgendwann Fehler.

Es ist ratsam, sich mit den Fingersätzen der Stücke zu befassen, solange man die Gelegenheit dazu hat. Man sollte den Gedankengang dahinter verstehen und sie nicht als selbstverständlich ansehen oder gar ignorieren!

In diesem Buch ist das Thema „Fingersatz" in mehrere Abschnitte untergliedert: Zuerst zeigen wir, wo eine Fünf-Finger-Lage verändert werden muss. Anschließend geben wir einen Fingersatz für einen Teil des Stückes an und empfehlen, die restlichen Takte mit einem Bleistift mit einem ähnlichen Fingersatz zu versehen. Dies wird zuerst bei zweistimmigen Stücken gemacht, dann bei der Einführung zweistimmiger Akkorde in der einen oder anderen Hand und schließlich bei dreistimmigen Akkorden und SATB-Voicings. Das letzte Kapitel enthält eine Mischung aus allem. Verschiedene Stile werden vorgestellt, u. a. der synkopische Jazz- und Swing-Stil sowie einige chromatische, modale und atonale Stücke. In diesen Stücken ist es wichtig, die Noten sorgfältig zu lesen, da es sein kann, dass sie anders klingen als erwartet.

Lernen hat zum Ziel, den Schüler auf seine Unabhängigkeit vorzubereiten und ihm so viel mit auf den Weg zu geben, dass er sich selbst aussuchen kann, was er spielen will. Daher ist es von Vorteil, wenn man Fingersätze versteht und vorausschauend lesen kann, um die notwendigen Positionswechsel rechtzeitig vorzunehmen. Die Spielstücke für Fortgeschrittene enthalten kaum oder gar keine Fingersätze. Daher muss ein routinierter Spieler verstehen, wie sie in der Praxis angewendet werden und in der Lage sein, selbst einen Fingersatz auszuarbeiten.

Das Buch besteht aus acht Lektionen. In jeder Lektion erwirbt der Spieler Schritt für Schritt sowohl ein theoretisches als auch ein praktisches Verständnis für die Prinzipien zur Ausarbeitung eines Fingersatzes. Auf diese Weise kommt der Pianist eines Tages auch mit einem Stück zurecht, das kaum oder keine Angaben zum Fingersatz hat und das er vorausschauend lesen muss, um den ökonomischsten und bequemsten Fingersatz anzuwenden und somit flüssig zu spielen. Hierbei sollte er sich eher auf sein Wissen und seine Erfahrung verlassen können als auf sein Glück.

**Lektion 1** hilft dem Spieler zunächst, eine Fünf-Finger-Lage zu „sehen" und den Finger auszuwählen, mit dem man die Phrase am besten beginnt. Anschließend wird anhand des Fingersatzes beim Spielen der Tonleiter gezeigt, wie dies mit einer minimalen Bewegung möglich ist. Man sollte einen Bleistift verwenden, um einen Fingersatz zu erarbeiten.
Alle Beispiele sind zweistimmig.

**Lektion 2** Lediglich der Beginn jedes zweistimmigen Stückes enthält Anregungen für einen Fingersatz. Die Spieler sollten sich unbedingt vorher einen Fingersatz überlegen und ihn mit Bleistift eintragen. Darüber hinaus wird in Lektion 2 betont, dass auch Oktavsprünge im Voraus geplant werden sollten. Enthaltene Stilrichtungen sind Swing und Ragtime. Außerdem kommt eine Ganztonleiter vor.

**Lektion 3** besteht aus längeren zweistimmigen Stücken, bei denen nur die ersten paar Takte eine Hilfestellung enthalten. Danach muss der Fingersatz gut überlegt werden, bevor man anfängt zu spielen.

**Lektion 4** enthält zweistimmige Akkorde und konzentriert sich hauptsächlich auf Terzen, Sexten und Oktaven.

In **Lektion 5** werden dreistimmige Akkorde sowie die besten Griffe dafür vorgestellt. Außerdem enthält das Kapitel Tonarten mit bis zu vier Kreuzen und Bes.

In **Lektion 6** geht es um das Spielen von vierstimmigen Akkorden (SATB)

**Lektion 7** enthält eine Vielzahl von Spielstilen und Tonarten.

**Lektion 8** bietet die Gelegenheit, das Spielen nach Akkordsymbolen zu erlernen: mit römischen Ziffern (die in der Harmonielehre verwendet werden), Generalbass (wie in der Barockmusik) und Akkordsymbolen (wie im Jazz und in der Popmusik).

# Section 1

## Section 1

### *Teil 1*

The brackets indicate a group of notes that remain in one hand position.
Decide, before you play, which finger is required for the start of each phrase.
Write in your fingering using only a pencil. Do this before you begin to play.
The left hand stays in one position.

Les crochets indiquent un groupe de notes pour lequel aucun changement de position des mains n'est nécessaire.
Avant de jouer, décidez quel doigt utiliser pour débuter chaque phrase. Inscrivez votre doigté en utilisant uniquement un crayon. Faites-le avant de commencer à jouer.
La main gauche conserve la même position.

Die Klammern geben eine Gruppe von Noten an, die in derselben Handposition gespielt werden.
Entscheide dich vor dem Spielen, mit welchem Finger du die jeweilige Phrase beginnen musst.
Trage deinen Fingersatz mit Bleistift ein, bevor du anfängst zu spielen.
Die linke Hand bleibt in einer Position.

**4.**

Only the starting fingering is given. Plot the remainder (and mark using a pencil) before you begin to play.

Seul le doigté de départ est indiqué. Imaginez les autres (et notez les au crayon) avant de commencer à jouer.

Hier ist nur am Anfang ein Fingersatz angegeben. Trage den restlichen Fingersatz (mit Bleistift) ein, bevor du anfängst zu spielen.

**5.**

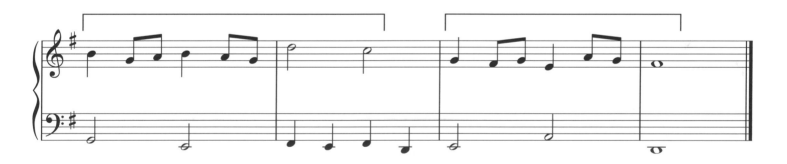

Before you can expect to play without written fingering it is important that you
a) understand the general principals and
b) learn to glance ahead to gauge the direction of each part in order to prepare to have the correct fingers available.

It is therefore recommended that you work out the best fingering for you and write it in in pencil first.

Avant de pouvoir imaginer commencer à jouer sans doigté écrit, il est important pour vous de :
a) comprendre les principes généraux
b) apprendre à anticiper la lecture pour évaluer la direction de chaque partie afin de pouvoir anticiper et avoir les doigts requis disponibles au bon moment.

C'est pourquoi nous recommandons de chercher le doigté qui vous convienne le mieux et de l'inscrire d'abord au crayon dans la partition.

Bevor du ohne angegebenen Fingersatz spielen kannst, ist es wichtig für dich,
a) die allgemeinen Prinzipien zu verstehen und
b) zu lernen vorausschauend zu lesen, um die Richtung der einzelnen Stimmen zu beurteilen und die richtigen Finger parat zu haben.

Daher ist es empfehlenswert, dass du den für dich besten Fingersatz herausarbeitest und ihn zuerst mit Bleistift einträgst.

Work out the fingering for the first 4 bars making use of the D major scale.

Déterminez le doigté des quatre premières mesures en utilisant la gamme de *ré* majeur.

Arbeite den Fingersatz für die ersten vier Takte heraus und wende dabei die D-Dur-Tonleiter an.

## 6.

Work out the fingering for the first 4 bars making use of the E♭ major scale.

Déterminez le doigté des quatre premières mesures en utilisant la gamme de *mi*♭ majeur.

Arbeite den Fingersatz für die ersten vier Takte heraus und wende dabei die Es-Dur-Tonleiter an.

## 6a.

Use the fingering for the D major scale. Use a pencil to write it in before you begin to play.

Utilisez le doigté de la gamme de *ré* majeur. Utilisez un crayon pour l'inscrire dans la partition avant de commencer à jouer.

Verwende den Fingersatz für die D-Dur-Tonleiter. Trage sie mit Bleistift ein, bevor du anfängst zu spielen.

## 7.

Now read the same notes but imagine the key of D flat major and adjust the fingering for that key.

À présent, lisez les mêmes notes, mais imaginez la tonalité de *ré* bémol majeur et ajustez les doigtés à cette tonalité.

Lies jetzt dieselben Noten, aber stell dir dabei die Tonart Des-Dur vor und passe den Fingersatz dieser Tonart an.

Only the essential fingering for the opening bars is given. Write in any other useful fingering.

Seuls les doigtés essentiels des premières mesures sont indiqués. Inscrivez tout autre doigté utile.

Hier ist nur der erforderliche Fingersatz für die Anfangstakte angegeben. Trage einen weiteren hilfreichen Fingersatz ein.

## 8.

With a swing feel

Avec une sensation de swing

Mit Swing-Feeling

Write in all essential fingering before you begin to play.

Inscrivez tous les doigtés essentiels avant de commencer à jouer.

Trage den erforderlichen Fingersatz ein, bevor du anfängst zu spielen.

## 9.

Base your fingering on the F major scale and appropriate arpeggios then pencil in your fingering.

Basez vos doigtés sur la gamme de *fa* majeur et sur les arpèges appropriés puis notez les au crayon.

Orientiere dich bei deinem Fingersatz an der F-Dur-Tonleiter und den entsprechenden Arpeggien und trage ihn dann mit Bleistift ein.

## 10.

As this needs a fast flowing tempo, using a pencil to work out the fingering would make for more fluent playing. Base your fingering on the A major scale.

Comme il faudra adopter un tempo rapide et coulant, l'utilisation d'un crayon pour déterminer les doigtés permettra une plus grande fluidité de jeu. Pour cela, appuyez-vous sur les doigtés de la gamme de *la* majeur.

Dieses Stück muss schnell und flüssig gespielt werden. Trage mit Bleistift den Fingersatz ein, mit dem du das Stück auf diese Weise spielen kannst. Orientiere dich bei deinem Fingersatz an der A-Dur-Tonleiter.

## 11.

**Allegro moderato**

The moves are now in the left hand while to right hand remain in a 5 note shape.

Les mouvements sont à présent à la main gauche tandis que la main droite conserve la même position.

Die Bewegungen werden jetzt mit der linken Hand ausgeführt, während die rechte in der Fünf-Finger-Lage bleibt.

## 12.

**Moderato**

*legato*

Use fingering for F major where applicable.

Utilisez le doigté de la gamme de *fa* majeur lorsqu'il est applicable.

Verwende den Fingersatz für die F-Dur-Tonleiter, wenn er passt.

## 13.

**Maestoso**

Continue to write in and plan your fingering before you begin to play.

Continuez à écrire et à planifier vos doigtés avant de commencer à jouer.

Überlege und trage deinen Fingersatz weiterhin ein, bevor du anfängst zu spielen.

## 14.

**Andantino**

Plan your fingering for each 2 bar phrase.

Planifiez vos doigtés pour chaque phrase de deux mesures.

Überlege dir einen Fingersatz für jede zweitaktige Phrase.

## 15.

**Grazioso**

Start afresh for each left hand phrase and aim to keep movement to a minimum.

Recommencez pour chaque phrase de la main gauche et tendez à limiter les mouvements au minimum.

Fang bei jeder Phrase für die linke Hand von vorn an und versuche, die Hand so wenig wie möglich zu bewegen.

## 16.

**Con moto**

Plan your fingering for the left hand around each 2 bar phrase.

Planifiez vos doigtés pour la main gauche environ toutes les phrases de deux mesures.

Überlege dir für jede zweitaktige Phrase einen Fingersatz für die linke Hand.

## 17.

**Cantabile**

Plan your fingering on the D major scale.

Calez vos doigtés sur la gamme de *ré* majeur.

Überlege dir einen Fingersatz in der D-Dur-Tonleiter.

## 18.

**Allegretto**

As far as is practical, base your finger-ing on each of the scale phrases.

Autant que possible, basez vos doigtés sur chacune des phrases en mouve-ment conjoint.

Orientiere dich bei deinem Fingersatz an den Tonleiterphrasen, soweit möglich.

### 19.

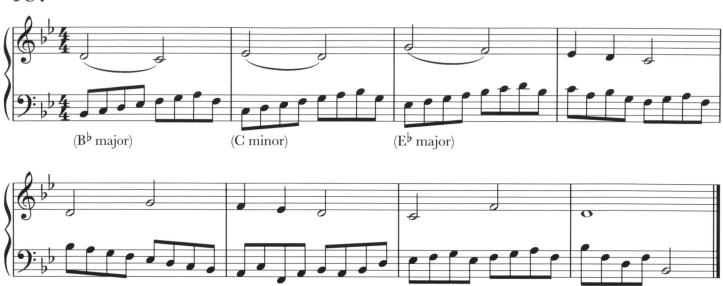

(B♭ major)   (C minor)   (E♭ major)

Parts of the fingering are given, but other phrases still need to be planned.

Certaines parties des doigtés sont in-diquées, mais d'autres phrases restent à déterminer.

Hier ist der Fingersatz teilweise angegeben; bei anderen Phrasen musst du ihn noch ergänzen.

### 20.

Use a similar fingering where the pattern occurs.

Utilisez un doigté similaire lorsque le motif réapparaît.

Verwende dort, wo das Pattern vorkommt, einen ähnlichen Finger-satz.

### 21.

Study the left hand fingering and continue with the same pattern where appropriate.

Étudiez le doigté de la main gauche et continuez selon le même schéma lorsque la partition s'y prête.

Hier solltest du dir den Fingersatz für die linke Hand anschauen und, wenn möglich, genauso weitermachen.

## 22.

Plan thoroughly before you begin to play.

Détaillez bien avant de commencer à jouer.

Überlege sorgfältig, bevor du anfängst zu spielen.

## 23.

# Section 2 – Fingering

## Section 2 – Doigtés

### *Teil 2 – Fingersatz*

In this section fingering is given for the first few bars only.
Using this as a guide, write in the remaining fingering before you begin to play.

In scale passages, wherever possible use the fingering for the appropriate key.

Dans cette partie, les doigtés sont indiqués uniquement pour les quelques mesures du début.
En les utilisant pour vous guider, écrivez les doigtés restants avant de commencer à jouer.

Dans les passages conjoints, lorsque c'est possible, utilisez les doigté de la gamme correspondante.

In dieser Lektion ist der Fingersatz nur für die ersten paar Takte angegeben. Verwende diesen Fingersatz als Anhaltspunkt und trage den restlichen Fingersatz ein, bevor du anfängst zu spielen.

In Tonleiterpassagen solltest du, wenn möglich, immer den Fingersatz für die jeweilige Tonart anwenden.

Before you begin to play, plot the remainder of the fingering and write it in using a pencil.

Avant de commencer à jouer, déterminez le reste du doigté et écrivez-le.

Bevor du anfängst zu spielen, solltest du den restlichen Fingersatz mit Bleistift eintragen.

## 24.

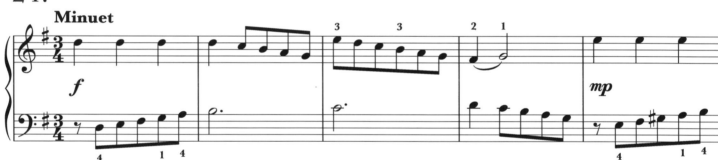

Fingering will change in different keys.

In B flat major:

Les doigtés changent en fonction des tonalités.

En *si* bémol majeur :

Der Fingersatz ändert sich je nach Tonart.

In B-Dur:

## 25.

In E major:

En *mi* majeur :

In E-Dur:

## 26.

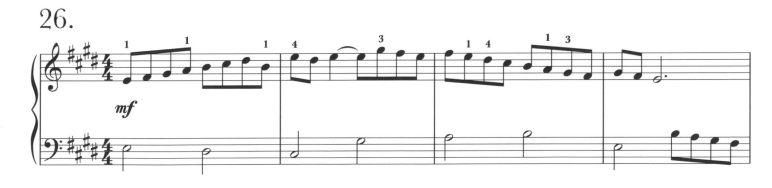

**27.**

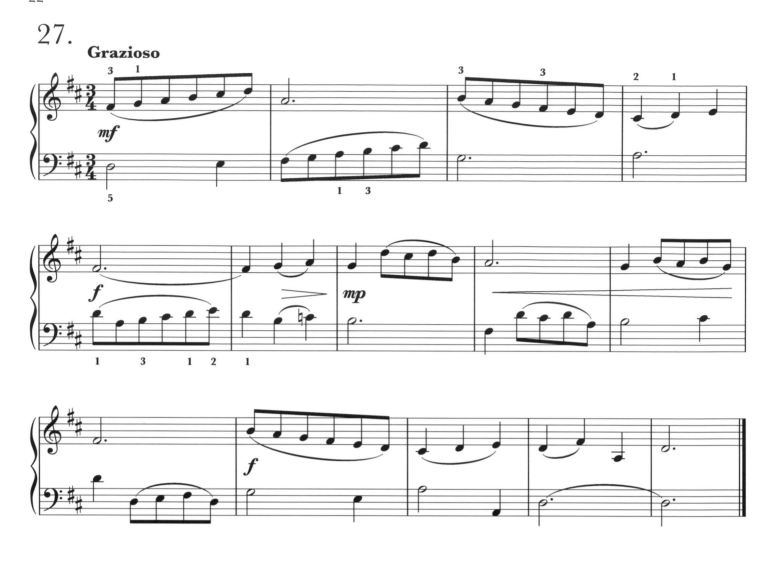

In passages containing sequences, use the same fingering wherever practical.

Dans les passages contenant des séquences, utilisez des doigtés identiques lorsque cela s'y prête.

In Passagen, die Sequenzen enthalten, solltest du, wenn möglich, denselben Fingersatz verwenden.

**28.**

In bars 3 and 5 it is more comfortable to use finger 2 on the F♯.

Aux mesures 3 et 5, il est plus confortable d'utiliser le 2e doigt sur le *fa♯*.

In Takt 3 und 5 ist es bequemer, das Fis mit dem 2. Finger zu spielen.

**29.**

Preparing for the octave.

Préparation de l'octave.

Vorbereitung auf die Oktave.

**30.**

**31.**

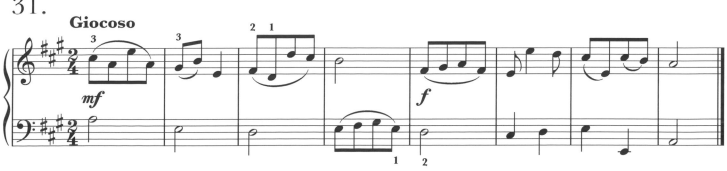

**32.**

**Stealthily**

**33.**

**Con brio**

**34.**

**Con spiritoso**

**35.**

In Ragtime style.          Dans le style d'un ragtime.          Im Ragtime-Stil.

**36.**

## 37.

Be careful to use only the fingering given.
This piece may sound a little strange at first as it is based on a whole tone scale.
Read carefully and play the notes exactly as written.

Veillez à utiliser uniquement les doigtés indiqués.
Cette pièce vous semblera peut-être un peu étrange à l'oreille au début, car elle repose sur une gamme par tons.
Lisez soigneusement et jouez les notes exactement telles qu'elles sont écrites.

Achte darauf, nur den angegebenen Fingersatz anzuwenden.
Dieses Stück klingt vielleicht etwas merkwürdig, da es eine Ganztonleiter als Grundlage hat.
Lies sorgfältig und spiele die Noten genauso wie notiert.

## 38.

Some essential fingering is given to begin with but it is recommended that the remaining fingering is written in before you begin to play.

Certains doigtés essentiels sont donnés au début, mais nous vous recommandons d'écrire les doigtés restants avant de commencer à jouer.

Hier ist ein Fingersatz für den Anfang angegeben. Trage den restlichen Fingersatz ein, bevor du anfängst zu spielen.

## 39.

## 40.

# Section 3 – Two-part exercises

## Section 3 – Exercises à deux voix

### *Teil 3 – Zweistimmige Übungen*

Plan your fingering carefully and write it in using a pencil. Preparing thoroughly will help towards a fluent reading.

Préparez soigneusement vos doigtés et inscrivez-les en utilisant un crayon. Une préparation détaillée vous aidera à obtenir une lecture fluide.

Überlege dir einen Fingersatz und trage ihn mit Bleistift ein. Eine gute Vorbereitung erleichtert das flüssige Lesen.

Some limited help is given but pencil in whatever else is necessary or useful.

L'aide qui vous est donnée ici est limitée, mais le crayon est utile, voire nécessaire pour le reste.

Hier werden zwar ein paar Hilfestellungen gegeben, aber du solltest alles eintragen, was dir notwendig bzw. nützlich erscheint.

## 41.

| A phrase that you have played previously with fingering is normally left blank, but play it using identical fingering.* | Une phrase que vous avez jouée précédemment avec un certain doigté ne comporte normalement pas de doigté, mais jouez-la en utilisant un doigté identique. * | Eine Phrase, die du vorher mit einem bestimmten Fingersatz gespielt hast, bleibt normalerweise leer, sollte aber mit demselben Fingersatz gespielt werden.* |

## 42.

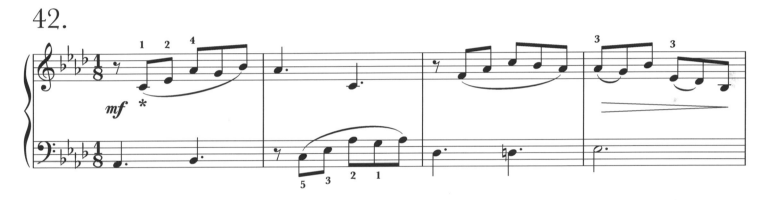

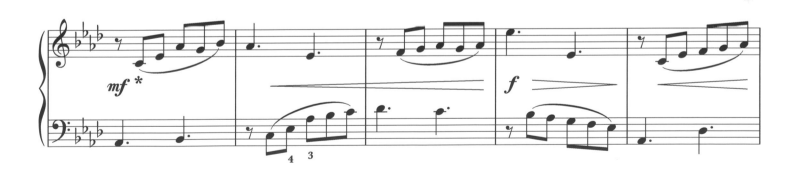

This will require careful and thorough planning if the style and fluency are to achieved.

Une préparation soigneuse et détaillée sera nécessaire pour obtenir style et fluidité.

Hier ist eine gründliche Vorbereitung erforderlich, wenn das Stück gemäß der Vortragsbezeichnung und flüssig gespielt werden soll.

**43.**

**44.**

**45.**

**Passacaglia**
**Adagio**

poco rall.

**46.**

**47.**

Slow swing                    Swing lent                    Langsamer Swing

48.

Before you play, prepare your fingering strategy mentally, and try to think
ahead and recall what you planned.
Unhurried – even quavers.

Avant de jouer, préparez mentalement
votre stratégie de doigtés et essayez
d'anticiper et de vous souvenir de ce
que vous avez prévu.
Sans presser – croches égales.

Überlege dir eine Fingersatzstrategie,
bevor du spielst und versuche, vorausschauend zu denken und dich an das
zu erinnern, was du dir überlegt hast.
Gemächlich – gerade Achtel.

## 49.

Work through this with your fingers
away from the keys. Write in only the
essential numbers.

Travaillez sans poser vos doigts sur les
touches. N'écrivez que les chiffres
essentiels.

Arbeite das Stück mit den Fingern
über den Tasten durch. Trage nur die
wichtigsten Zahlen ein.

## 50.

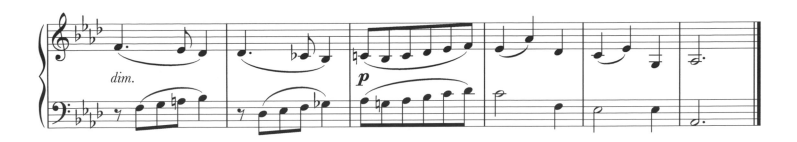

Slow ballad 16-beat style.

Dans le style d'une ballade lente à 16 temps.

Langsame 16-Beat-Ballade.

51.

Plan this carefully as you will have to play some black notes with your thumbs and change fingers on some notes too.

Préparez ce passage avec soin, car vous devrez jouer quelques notes noires avec votre pouce tout en effectuant également quelques changements de doigts sur certaines notes.

Der Fingersatz für dieses Stück sollte gut durchdacht sein, da du ein paar schwarze Tasten mit den Daumen spielen und bei einigen Noten den Finger wechseln musst.

## 52.

Easy swing  [♫ = ♩♪]        Swing facile  [♫ = ♩♪]        Easy  [♫ = ♩♪]

## 53.

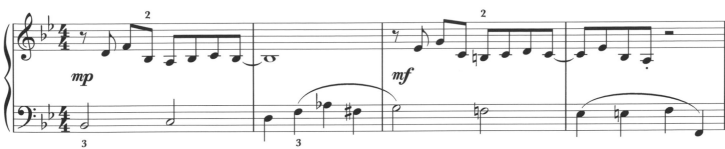

The reader is free to add their own dynamics depending on the direction of the music.

Le lecteur est libre d'ajouter ses propres indications de dynamique en fonction de l'esprit de la musique.

Du kannst je nach Verlauf der Melodie eigene dynamische Zeichen einfügen.

## 54.

**Larghetto**

Dynamic shading is at the discretion of the player.

La couleur dramatique est à la discrétion de l'instrumentiste.

Die dynamischen Abstufungen bleiben dem Spieler überlassen.

## 55.

**Resoluto**

With this slow tempo it should be possible to play at sight. It will be vital to watch which direction the hands are moving.

Avec ce tempo lent, il devrait être possible de jouer à vue. Il sera vital d'observer la direction des mains.

Bei diesem langsamen Tempo sollte es möglich sein, das Stück vom Blatt zu spielen. Es ist wichtig, darauf zu achten, in welche Richtung sich die Hände bewegen.

## 56.

**Larghetto**

57.

## 58.

**Ragtime**

Notice the double sharps in these next two pieces.

Notez les doubles-dièses figurant dans les deux prochains morceaux.

Beachte die Doppelkreuze in den beiden nächsten Stücken.

## 59.

## 60.

# Section 4 – Two-note chords
## Section 4 – Accords de deux notes
### *Teil 4 – Zweistimmige Akkorde*

Fingering for groups of consecutive 3rds:

Doigtés de groupes de tierces consécutives :

Fingersatz für Gruppen aus aufeinanderfolgenden Terzen:

Fingering for groups of 6ths is more dependent on hand size and stretch, but ideally:

Les doigtés des groupes de sixtes dépendent davantage de la taille de la main et de l'extension des doigts, mais idéalement :

Der Fingersatz für Gruppen aus Sexten hängt zwar davon ab, wie groß deine Hände sind und wie weit du die Finger spreizt, lautet idealerweise jedoch folgendermaßen:

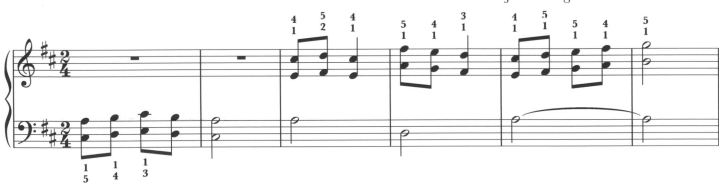

Similarly with octaves:

Il en va de même pour les octaves :

Genauso bei Oktaven:

44

Use the phrase marks and slurs to
guide your fingering.

Utilisez les indications de phrasé et les
liaisons pour guider vos doigtés.

## 61.

Don't forget to prepare the left hand
octaves.

N'oubliez pas de préparer les octaves
de la main gauche.

Vergiss nicht, die Oktaven in der
linken Hand vorzubereiten.

## 62.

Think about how to finger the consecutive 3rds and prepare the left
hand octaves correctly.
Take care! B major and double
sharps.

Pensez aux doigtés des tierces consécutives et préparez correctement
les octaves de la main gauche.
Attention ! *Si* majeur et doubles-
dièses.

Überlege, wie du die aufeinanderfolgenden Terzen greifen kannst und
bereite dich gut auf die Oktaven in
der linken Hand vor.
Achtung: H-Dur und Doppelkreuze.

## 63.

Prepare your fingering according to
the phrasing.

Préparez vos doigtés en fonction du
phrasé.

Bereite deinen Fingersatz
entsprechend der Phrasierung vor.

## 64.

## 65.

**Allegretto**

Plan your fingering with care whether written in or memorised.

Préparez soigneusement vos doigtés qu'ils soient écrits ou mémorisés.

Plane deinen Fingersatz immer sorgfältig, ob du ihn nun notierst oder auswendig lernst.

## 66.

**Poco allegro**

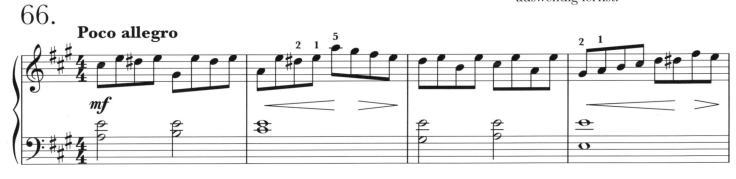

Be careful with the fingering of the inner parts.

Veillez aux doigtés des voix intermédiaires.

Sei beim Fingersatz der Mittelstimmen besonders sorgfältig.

## 67.

## 68.

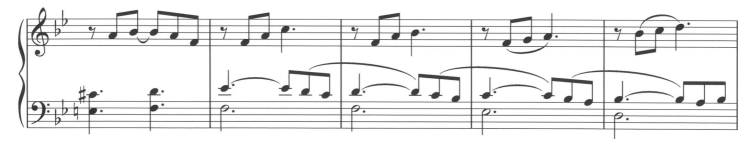

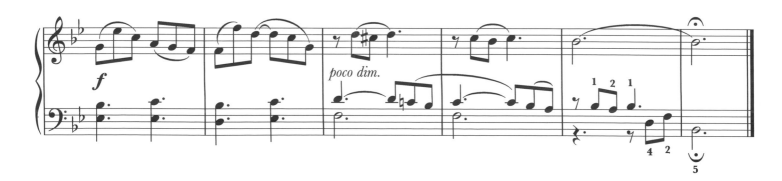

69.

70.

Make sure the fingering is prepared for the legato 'walking bass'.

Veillez à ce que les doigtés soient prêts pour le *legato* de la *walking-bass*.

Achte darauf, dass der Fingersatz zum *legato* gespielten „Walking Bass" passt.

## 71.

**72.**

75.

**76.**

Allegro moderato

**77.**

Andantino

# Section 5 – Three-note chords

## Section 5 – Accords de trois notes

### *Teil 5 – Dreistimmige Akkorde*

Plan before you play which finger to start each left hand phrase with.

Avant de jouer, déterminez par quel doigt commencer chaque phrase.

Überlege vor dem Spielen, mit welchem Finger du die Phrasen für die linke Hand beginnst.

**78.**

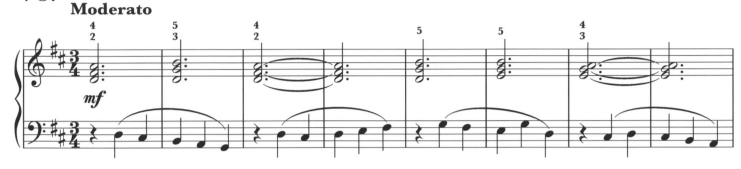

Prepare the 'shape' of the chord before you reach it.

Préparez la « forme » de l'accord avant de le jouer.

Bereite die Handhaltung für den Akkord vor, bevor du ihn spielst.

**79.**

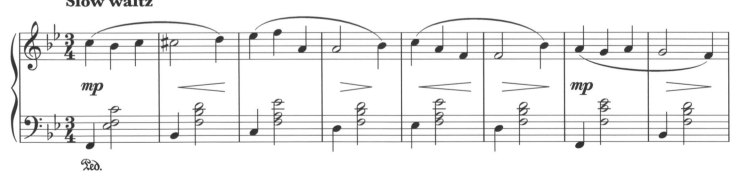

54

Sensitive use of the sustain pedal and fingering the chords in pairs will help achieve a smooth result.
It may be necessary to use the 4th finger on some 2nd inv. chords.

Une utilisation subtile de la pédale forte et les doigtés des accords vous aideront à obtenir un résultat plus doux. Il pourra être nécessaire d'utiliser le 4e doigt sur certains accords de seconde renversés.

Ein gefühlvoller Einsatz des Sostenutopedals und das Spielen der Akkorde mit zwei Fingern tragen dazu bei, dass das Stück flüssig gespielt wird. Beim Spielen der zweiten Umkehrung muss manchmal der 4. Finger zu benutzt werden.

A different style of left hand accompaniment. It is recommended to study the left hand chords before you play.

Accompagnement de style différent à la main gauche. Il est préférable d'étudier les accords de la main gauche avant de jouer.

Ein anderer Begleitstil mit der linken Hand. Du solltest dir auf jeden Fall die Akkorde für die linke Hand anschauen, bevor du spielst.

**83.**

Scan the entire piece before you play. Notice the double sharps as well as the left hand chords.

Passez en revue la pièce dans son entier avant de jouer. Notez les doubles-dièses ainsi que les accords de la main gauche.

Schau dir das ganze Stück an, bevor du spielst. Beachte die Doppelkreuze sowie die Akkorde für die linke Hand.

**84.**

**85.**

It would be advisable to work out the left hand legato fingering before you play.

Il est préférable de déterminer le doigté du *legato* de la main gauche avant de jouer.

Du solltest den *Legato*-Fingersatz für die linke Hand herausarbeiten, bevor du spielst.

## 86.

Make sure the rhythm is secure before you play.

Assurez-vous que le rythme est en place avant de jouer.

Achte darauf, dass du den Rhythmus beherrschst, bevor du spielst.

**88.**

**89.**

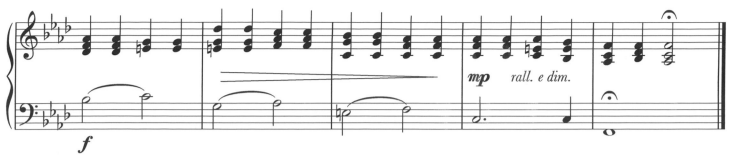

**90.** **Poco adagio**

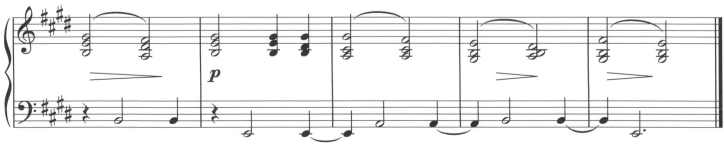

# Section 6 – Four-part chords (SATB)

Section 6 – Accords à quatre voix (SATB)

*Teil 6 – Vierstimmige Akkorde (SATB)*

Always aim to play legato and be guided by phrase marks and slurs.

Visez toujours un jeu *legato* et laissez-vous guider par les indications et les liaisons de phrasé.

Versuche immer, *legato* zu spielen und nimm die Phrasierungszeichen und Bindebögen als Leitfaden.

**91.**

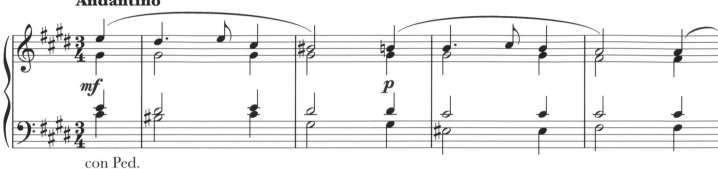

**92.**

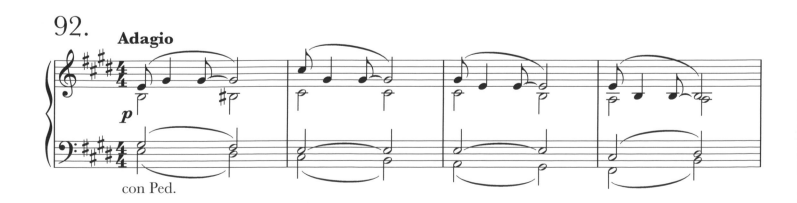

'Legato fingering' in chordal playing sometimes entails finger changes on held notes.

Lorsqu'il s'agit de jouer en accords, le « doigté *legato* » implique parfois des changements de doigts sur les notes tenues.

Ein „*Legato*-Fingersatz" beim Akkordspiel beinhaltet manchmal Fingerwechsel auf gehaltenen Noten.

## 93.
### Solennemente

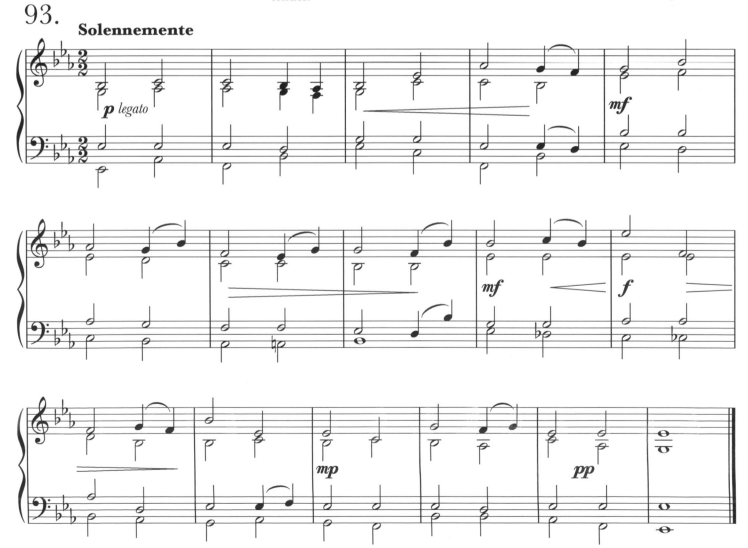

Medium waltz tempo          Tempo moyen de valse          Mittelschnelles Walzertempo

**94.**

Joyfully          Gaiement          Fröhlich

**95.**

96.

**Sentimentale**

64

With so many accidentals it is worth-
while miming with your fingers to
feel the right chord shapes.

En présence d'autant d'altérations
accidentelles, il vaut la peine de mimer
avec vos doigts pour vous imprégner
de la forme des accords.

Bei so vielen Vorzeichen ist es ange-
bracht, erst einmal nur so zu tun, als
würdest du spielen, um ein Gefühl
für die richtigen Akkordgriffe zu
bekommen.

With a gentle lilt

Avec un entrain modéré

Sanft wiegend

# Section 7 – Various styles and tonalities

## Section 7 – Tonalités et styles variés

### *Teil 7 – Verschiedene Spielstile und Tonarten*

Remember, it is the unfamiliar that catches us out when reading. Unexpected chord shapes and harmonies, unusual textures and tonalities, accidentals, rhythms and keys. Always scan the entire piece before you play to help be aware of the unexpected or unusual.

Souvenez-vous, ce sont les éléments dont nous ne sommes pas familiers qui nous prennent au dépourvu au moment de la lecture : harmonies et accords inattendus, textures, altérations accidentelles, rythmes et tonalités inhabituelles. Passez toujours toute la partition en revue avant de la jouer afin d'avoir conscience de la présence d'éléments inattendus ou inhabituels.

Beim Lesen wird man immer wieder von ungewöhnlichen Dingen überrascht. Unerwartete Akkordgriffe und Harmonien, ungewöhnliche Klangstrukturen, Tonalitäten, Vorzeichen, Rhythmen und Tonarten. Gehe immer das gesamte Stück kurz durch, bevor du spielst, damit du unerwartete bzw. ungewöhnliche Aspekte wahrnimmst.

99.

**100.**

**102.**

**103.**

Dynamic shaping at the players discretion.

L'élaboration dynamique est à la
discrétion de l'interprète.

Die dynamische Gestaltung bleibt
dem Spieler überlassen.

## 104.

## 105.

Even quavers           Croches égales           gerade Achtel

106.

**Moderato**

With a driving beat          Avec entrain          Mit treibendem Beat

## 107.

*repeat to fade*

# Section 8 – Appendix
## Section 8 – Annexe
### *Teil 8 – Anhang*

| | | |
|---|---|---|
| Apart from musical notation, these harmonies can be indicated in three other ways. | Outre la notation musicale, ces harmonies peuvent être indiquées de trois autres manières. | Neben der Notenschrift können diese Harmonien auch auf drei weitere Arten dargestellt werden. |
| The conventional way is by key related Roman numbers. | La manière conventionnelle fonctionne avec des chiffres romains en rapport avec la tonalité. | Die herkömmliche Schreibweise besteht aus römischen Ziffern, die sich auf die Tonart beziehen. |
| In Baroque music the figured bass uses numbers to show which notes above the bass notes need to be played. A bass note without figures indicates a root position chord $\left(\begin{smallmatrix}5\\3\end{smallmatrix}\right)$. | Dans la musique baroque, la basse figurée utilise des chiffres pour désigner les notes qui doivent être jouées au-dessus de la basse. Il n'y a pas de chiffre indiquant la position fondamentale de l'accord. | In der Barockmusik werden für den Generalbass Ziffern verwendet, um zu zeigen, welche Noten über dem Basston gespielt werden müssen. Keine Ziffer bedeutet, dass ein Akkord in der Grundstellung gespielt wird. |

| | | |
|---|---|---|
| 6 – a first inversion | 6 – premier renversement | 6 – erste Umkehrung |
| $\begin{smallmatrix}6\\4\end{smallmatrix}$ – a second inversion | $\begin{smallmatrix}6\\4\end{smallmatrix}$ – deuxième renversement | $\begin{smallmatrix}6\\4\end{smallmatrix}$ – zweite Umkehrung |
| $\begin{smallmatrix}6\\4\\2\end{smallmatrix}$ – a third inversion of a 7th chord | $\begin{smallmatrix}6\\4\\2\end{smallmatrix}$ – troisième renversement d'un accord de 7e | $\begin{smallmatrix}6\\4\\2\end{smallmatrix}$ – dritte Umkehrung eines Septakkords |
| $\begin{smallmatrix}5\\3\end{smallmatrix}$ – a root position (usually following a 6) | $\begin{smallmatrix}5\\3\end{smallmatrix}$ – accord fondamental (généralement précédé d'un 6) | $\begin{smallmatrix}5\\3\end{smallmatrix}$ – Grundstellung (meist nach einer 6) |
| Jazz and popular music use chord names (e.g. Am – G$^7$ – C) | Le jazz et la musique populaire utilisent les noms des accords (par ex. *lam – sol$^7$ – do*) | In der Jazz- und Popmusik werden Akkordsymbole verwendet (z. B. Am – G$^7$ – C) |

| | | |
|---|---|---|
| Roman numerals Chiffres romains Römische Ziffern | Figured Bass Basse figurée Generalbass | Jazz chords Accords de jazz Jazzakkorde |

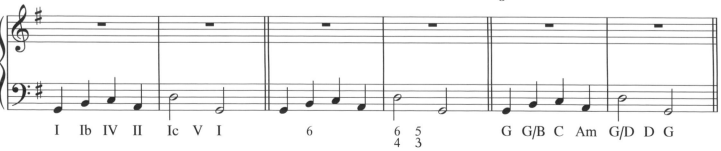

I  Ib  IV  II  Ic  V  I          6          $\begin{smallmatrix}6\\4\end{smallmatrix}$ $\begin{smallmatrix}5\\3\end{smallmatrix}$          G  G/B  C  Am  G/D  D  G

Some basic harmonic progressions –
SATB cadences:

Quelques progressions harmoniques
de base – cadences SATB :

Einige gängige Akkordfolgen –
SATB-Kadenzen:

The Perfect Cadence
Key: G major

La cadence parfaite
Tonalité : *sol* majeur

Authentische Kadenz
Tonart: G-Dur

The Interrupted Cadence
Key: G major

La cadence rompue
Tonalité : *sol* majeur

Trugschluss
Tonart: G-Dur

The Imperfect Cadence
Key: G major

La cadence imparfaite
Tonalité : *sol* majeur

Halbschluss
Tonart: G-Dur

The Plagal Cadence
Key: G major

La cadence plagale
Tonalité : *sol* majeur

Plagaler Schluss
Tonart: G-Dur

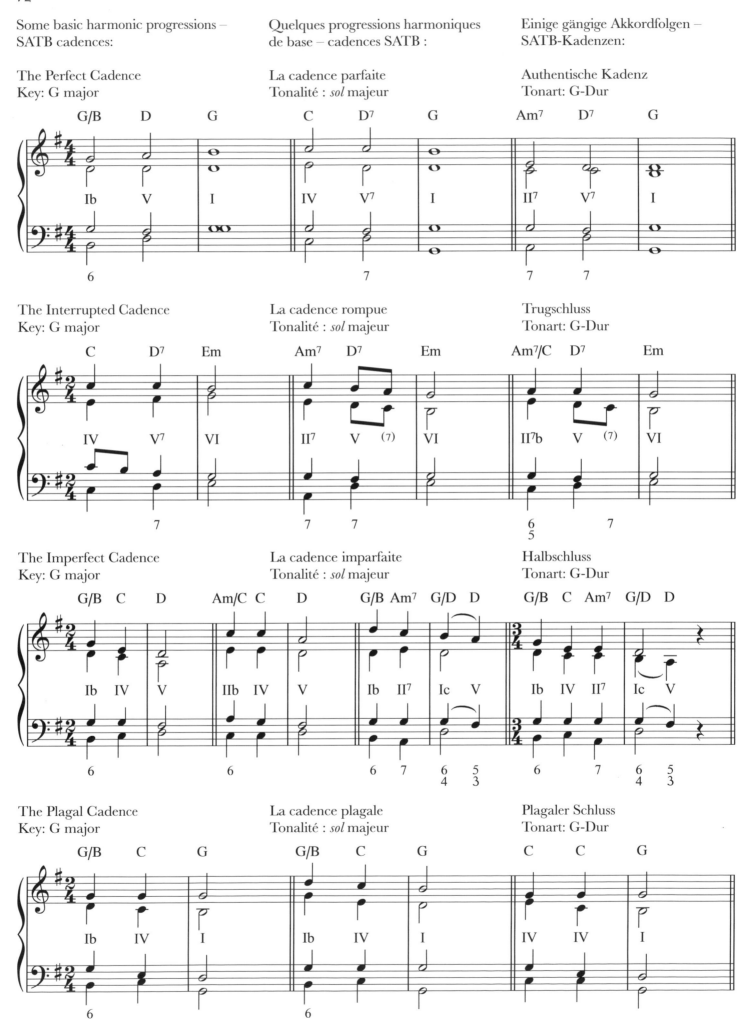

| The Figured Bass | La basse figurée | Generalbass |
|---|---|---|
| Add inner parts.<br>Key: G major | Ajoutez les voix intermédiaires.<br>Tonalité : *sol* majeur | Füge die Mittelstimmen hinzu.<br>Tonart: G-Dur |

## 108.

| Key: G major | Tonalité : *sol* majeur | Tonart: G-Dur |
|---|---|---|

## 109.

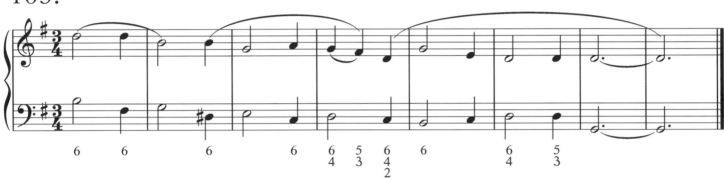

| Key: G major | Tonalité : *sol* majeur | Tonart: G-Dur |
|---|---|---|

## 110.

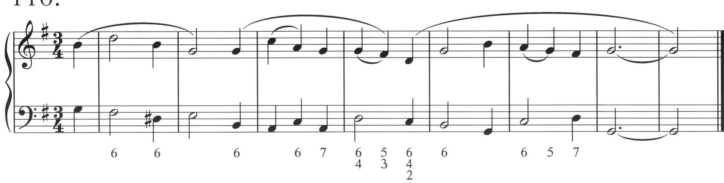

| Add upper part or parts. Best to keep outer parts in contrary motion.<br>Key: E minor | Ajoutez une ou des voix au-dessus. Il est préférable que les voix extrêmes soient en mouvement contraire.<br>Tonalité : *mi* mineur | Füge eine oder mehrere Oberstimmen hinzu. Am besten bilden die Außenstimmen eine Gegenbewegung.<br>Tonart: e-Moll |

## 111.

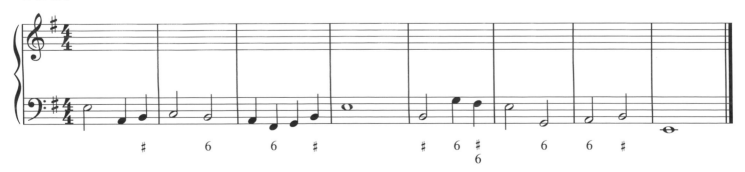

Add simple harmonies to this bass line, giving it the same rhythm.
Key: A minor

Ajoutez des harmonies simples à cette ligne de basse en conservant le même rythme.
Tonalité : *la mineur*

Füge einfache Harmonien zu dieser Basslinie hinzu und behalte den Rhythmus bei.
Tonart: a-Moll

## 112.

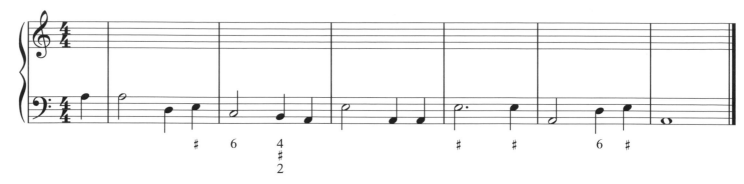

Complete the inner parts and continue the melodic line.
Key: F major

Complétez les parties intermédiaires et poursuivez la ligne mélodique.
Tonalité : *fa majeur*

Vervollständige die Mittelstimmen und führe die Melodiestimme fort.
Tonart: F-Dur

## 113.

Chord using Roman Numerals

Accord utilisant des chiffres romains

Akkord mit römischen Ziffern

Complete the chords by adding the two inner parts (S.A.T.B.).
Key: E♭ major

Complétez les accords en ajoutant les deux parties intermédiaires (S.A.T.B.).
Tonalité : *mi♭ majeur*

Vervollständige die Akkorde, indem du zwei Mittelstimmen hinzufügst (S.A.T.B.).
Tonart: Es-Dur

## 114.

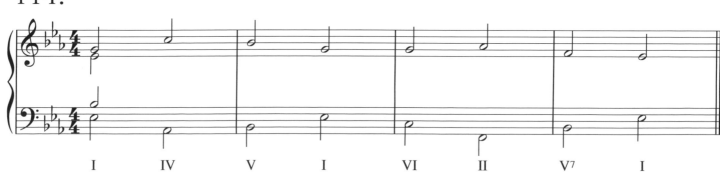

Add the remaining chords in a similar style.
Key: F major

Ajoutez les accords restants dans un style similaire.
Tonalité : *fa* majeur

Füge die restlichen Akkorde im selben Stil hinzu.
Tonart: F-Dur

## 115.

I     IV     V     I     VI     Ib

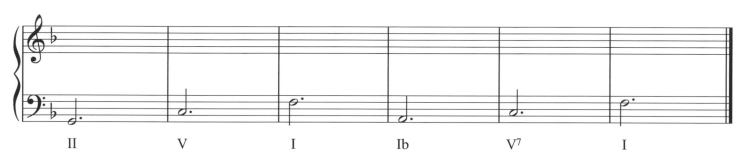

II     V     I     Ib     V⁷     I

Add the left hand chords to this melody continuing the style.
Key: D major

Ajoutez les accords de la main gauche à cette mélodie en restant dans le même style.
Tonalité : *ré* majeur

Füge die Akkorde für die linke Hand im selben Stil zur Melodie hinzu.
Tonart: D-Dur

## 116.

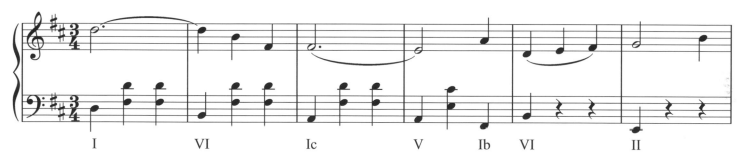

I     VI     Ic     V     Ib    VI     II

V     V⁷d     Ib     IV     V     V⁷d

Ib     VI     II     V     I

Continue the arpeggio figures according to the chords indicated.
Key: G minor

Continuez les figures d'arpèges en fonction des accords indiqués.
Tonalité : *sol* mineur

Führe die Arpeggio-Figuren entsprechend den angegebenen Akkorden weiter.
Tonart: g-Moll

## 117.

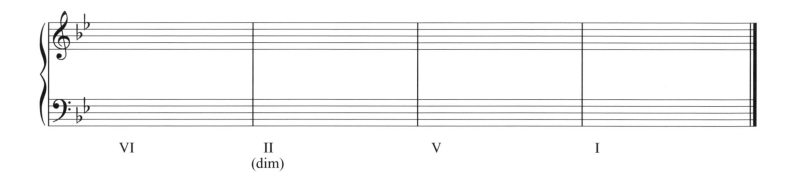

Continue this 'vamp' style accompaniment.
Key: F major

Poursuivez cet accompagnement dans le style « vamp ».
Tonalité : *fa* majeur

Führe diese Begleitung im „Vamp"-Stil fort.
Tonart: F-Dur

## 118.

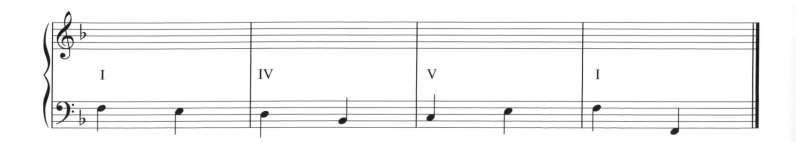

77

Complete these chords in 4 part (S.A.T.B.) harmony.
Key: C minor

Complétez ces accords en les harmonisant à quatre voix (S.A.T.B.).
Tonalité : *do* mineur

Vervollständige die Akkorde, so dass sie vierstimmig werden (S.A.T.B.).
Tonart: c-Moll

## 119.

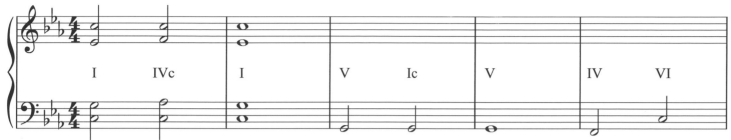

Continue using the suggested chords.
Key: B minor

Continuez en utilisant les accords suggérés.
Tonalité : *si* mineur

Fahre mit den vorgeschlagenen Akkorden fort.
Tonart: h-Moll

## 120.

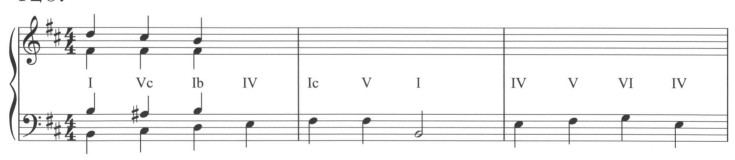

Complete the broad arpeggio figure throughout the left hand.

Key: B minor

Complétez la grande figure arpégée de la main gauche.

Tonalité : *si* mineur

Vervollständige die weit gedehnte Arpeggio-Figur durchgängig für die linke Hand.

Tonart: h-Moll

## 121.

Continue the style of broken chords to the given symbols to form an accompaniment.

Key: G major

Continuez dans le style d'accords brisés en fonction des symboles indiqués pour former un accompagnement.

Tonalité : *sol* majeur

Führe den Stil gebrochener Akkorde zu den angegebenen Symbolen fort, um eine Begleitung zu bilden.

Tonart: G-Dur

## 122.

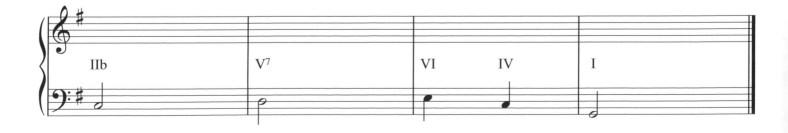

Complete the inner harmonies.
Key: E♭ major

Complétez les harmonies intermédi-aires.
Tonalité : *mi*♭ majeur

Vervollständige die Mittelstimmen.
Tonart: Es-Dur

## 123.

VI  II  V  Ib  IV  II  Ic  V  V⁷b  Ib  IV  Ib  II⁷  Ib  IV  V⁷  VI  II  IIb  V⁷  V⁷c  I

Jazz and Pop Chords

Accords de jazz et de pop

Jazz- und Pop-Akkorde

Study and play this chord progression and notice the cycle of fifths.

Jouez et étudiez cette progression d'ac-cords et remarquez bien les cycles de quintes.

Spiele und analysiere die Akkordfolge und beachte den Quintenzirkel

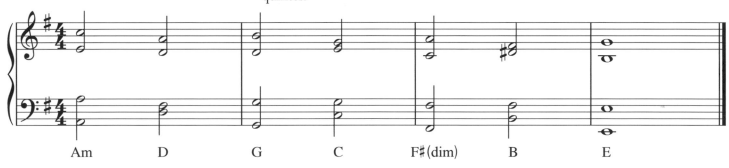

Am    D    G    C    F♯(dim)    B    E

Notice how the addition of the 7th gives a smoother progression.

Notez comment l'ajout de la 7e confère davantage de douceur à la progression.

Beachte, dass die Akkordfolge durch den hinzugefügten Septakkord flüs-siger wird.

Am⁷    D    Gmaj⁷    C    F♯m7♭5    B    Em
[Am/F♯]

Now with 7th resolving onto 7th in the same progression.

À présent, avec des 7e se résolvant dans des 7e selon la même progres-sion.

Und jetzt wird der Septakkord in derselben Akkordfolge mit einem Septakkord aufgelöst.

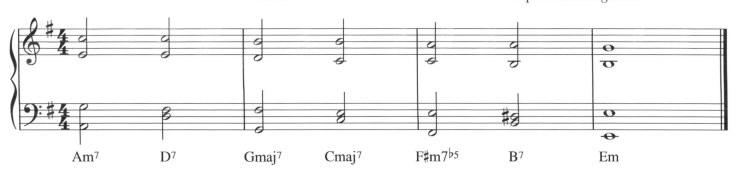

Am⁷    D⁷    Gmaj⁷    Cmaj⁷    F♯m7♭5    B⁷    Em

1. Play block chords on the first beat. Play only the 3rd and 7th or root and 3rd in each case.

2. Make the right hand chords form rhythmic patterns.
e.g.

1. Plaquez les accords sur le premier temps. Dans chaque cas, jouez uniquement la 3ce et la 7e ou la fondamentale et la 3ce.

2. Appliquez des motifs rythmiques aux accords de la main droite,
par ex. :

1. Spiele Blockakkorde auf der Eins. Spiele jedes Mal nur Terz und Septime oder Grundton und Terz.

2. Bilde aus den rhythmischen Pattern Akkorde für die rechte Hand,
z. B.

## 124.

Add chords below this slow, ballad style melody. Maintain the steady 4 chords per bar as given.
Chords: Diminished 7th, flat 5th and optional 13th.

Ajoutez les accords sous cette mélodie lente dans le style d'une ballade. Veillez à maintenir la stabilité de la succession de quatre accords par mesure telle qu'elle est indiquée. Accords : 7e diminuée, 5te diminuée et 13e facultative.

Schreibe Akkorde unter die folgende langsame Melodie im Balladenstil. Behalte die angegebenen vier Akkorde pro Takt bei.
Akkorde: verminderter Septakkord, verminderte Quinte und optionale Tredezime

## 125.

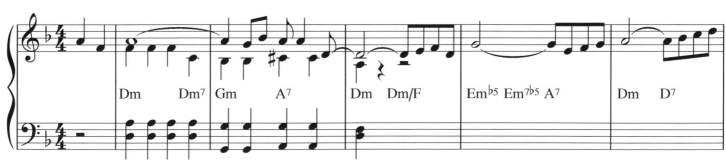

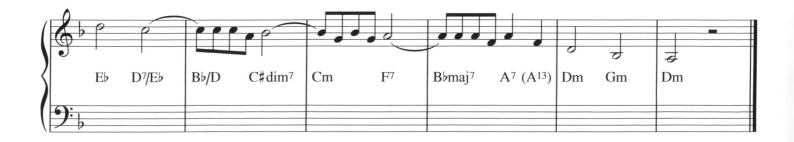

Continue with this arpeggio style left hand using the chords given. Chords: Major, minor and diminished 7ths.

Continuez avec la main gauche arpégée en utilisant les accords indiqués. Accords : 7e majeures, mineures et diminuées.

Mach mit der linken Hand im Arpeggio-Stil weiter und verwende dabei die angegebenen Akkorde. Akkorde: Dur-, Moll- und verminderte Septakkorde.

## 126.

**Andante**

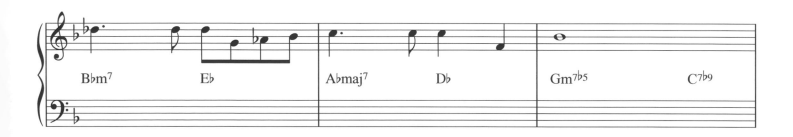

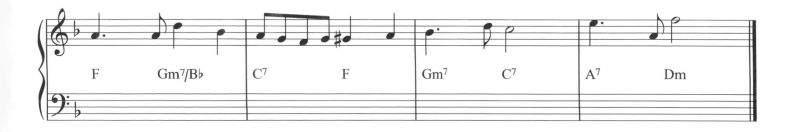

82

Complete playing the given chords
to the rhythm indicated.
Chords: 1st inversions (e.g. Dm/F)
and sharpened 5ths.
Relaxed tempo and even quavers

Complétez en jouant les accords
donnés dans le rythme indiqué : 1er
renversement (par ex *rém/fa*) et
quintes augmentées.
Accords : 1er renversement (par ex.
*rém/fa*) et 5re augmentée.
Tempo détendu et croches régulières

Spiele die angegebenen Akkorde zum
angegebenen Rhythmus weiter.
Akkorde: erste Umkehrung (z. B.
Dm/F) und übermäßige Quinte
Entspanntes Tempo und gerade
Achtel

## 127.

Gm/Bb    A⁷         Fm/Ab    G⁷

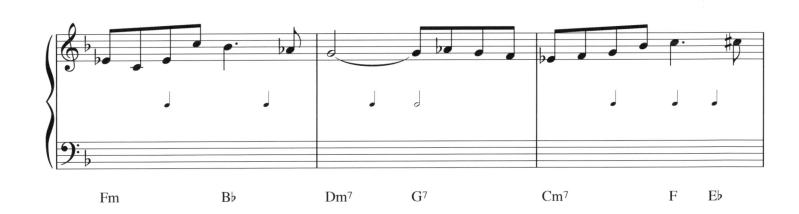

Fm       Bb      Dm⁷     G⁷      Cm⁷      F   Eb

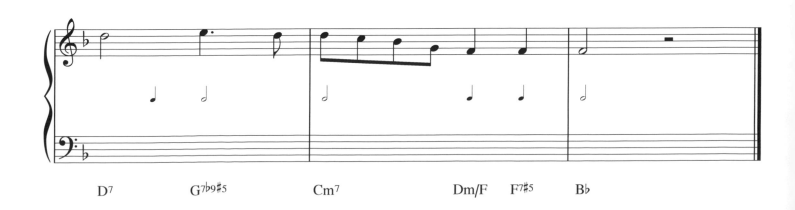

D⁷      G⁷♭9♯5      Cm⁷      Dm/F   F⁷♯5    Bb

Continue filling in the chords in a
similar 'slow ballad' style.
Chords: Flat 5ths and 9ths.

Continuez à remplir les accords dans
le même style de ballade lente.
Accords : 5tes diminuées et de 9e.

Trage weitere Akkorde im selben Stil
einer langsamen Ballade ein.
Akkorde: Verminderte Quinten und
Nonen.

## 128.

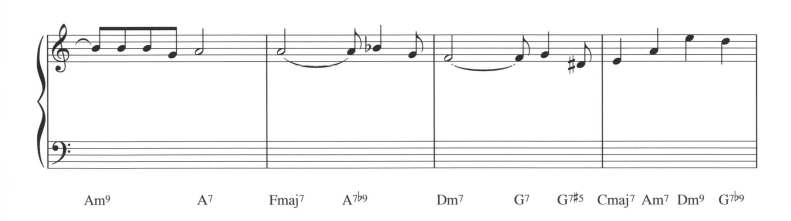

Using Diminished 7ths, 11ths and 13ths.

Usage des 7e diminuées, 11e et 13e.

Verwende verminderte Septakkorde, Undezimen und Tredezimen.

**129.**

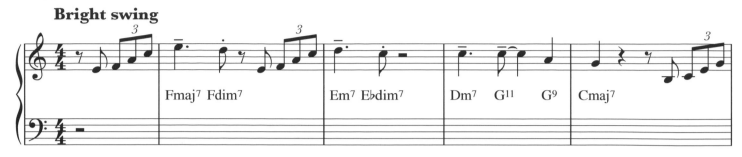

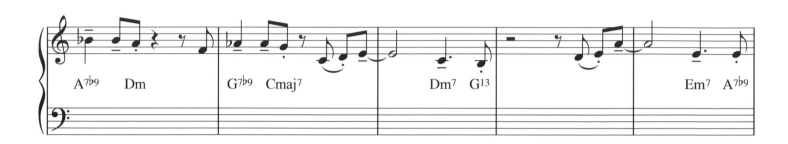

Straight 4 – even quavers

Quarte juste – croches égales

Straight 4 – gerade Achtel

**130.**